sax

Now yo
alto saxophone
specially recorded arrangements

TAKE
THE
LEAD

Swing

alto
saxophone

IMP

International MUSIC Publications

International Music Publications Limited
Griffin House 161 Hammersmith Road London W6 8BS England

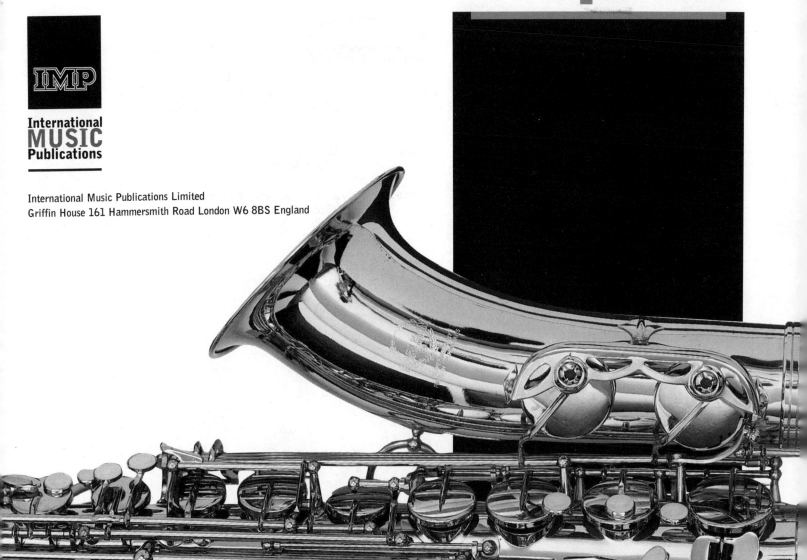

Series Editors: Sadie Cook and Miranda Steel

Editorial, production and recording: Artemis Music Limited
Design and production: Space DPS Limited

Published 2000

International MUSIC Publications

IMP

International Music Publications Limited

England: Griffin House
161 Hammersmith Road
London W6 8BS

Germany: Marstallstr. 8
D-80539 München

Denmark: Danmusik
Vognmagergade 7
DK1120 Copenhagen K

Carisch

Italy: Via Campania 12
20098 San Giuliano Milanese
Milano

Spain: Magallanes 25
28015 Madrid

France: 20 Rue de la Ville-l'Eveque
75008 Paris

alto saxophone

TAKE THE LEAD

In the Book...

On the CD...

Demonstration

Backing

Chattanooga Choo Choo

Music by Harry Warren

Demonstration

Backing

I've Got A
Gal In Kalamazoo

Music by Harry Warren

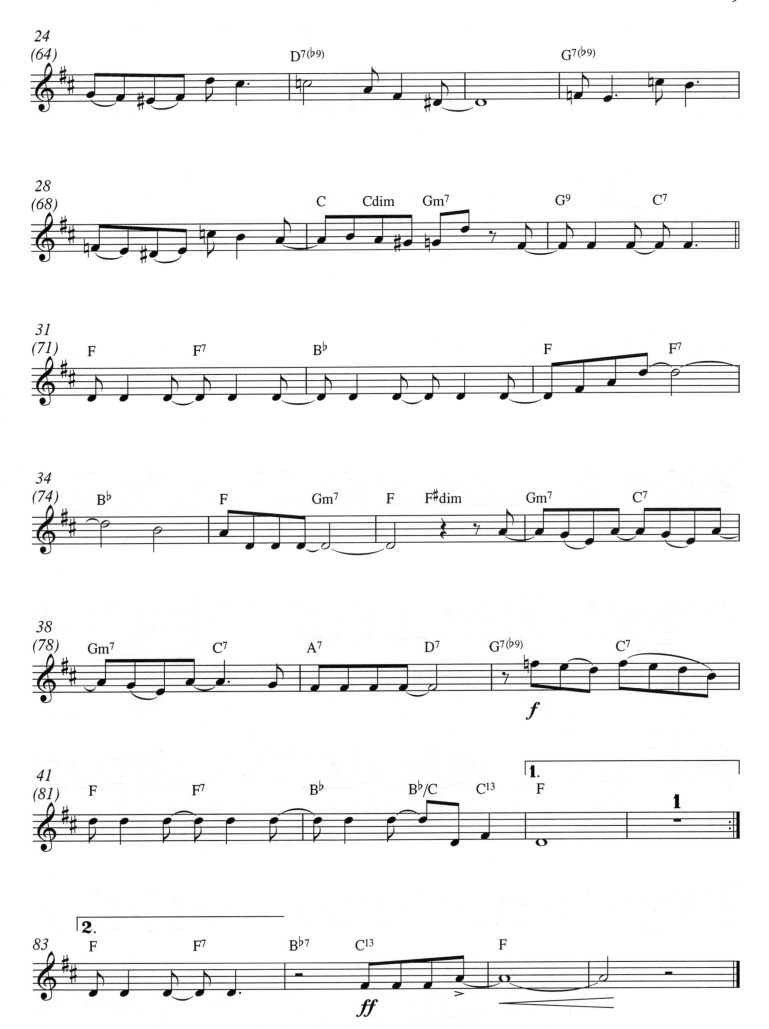

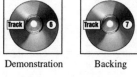

Demonstration　Backing

In The Mood

Music by Joe Garland

Demonstration

Backing

It Don't Mean A Thing
(If It Ain't Got That Swing)

Music by Duke Ellington

Bright swing

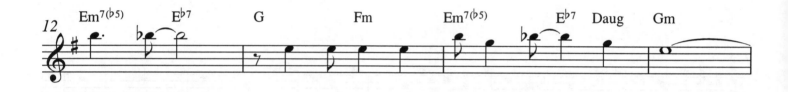

Demonstration

Backing

Choo Choo Ch'Boogie

Words and Music by Denver Darling,
Milton Gabler and Vaughn Horton

Moderate boogie woogie tempo

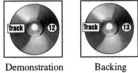

Demonstration   Backing

Jersey Bounce

Music by Tiny Bradshaw
and Bobby Plater

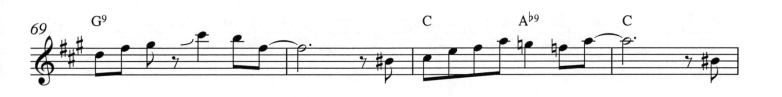

Demonstration

Backing

Pennsylvania 6-5000

Music by Jerry Gray

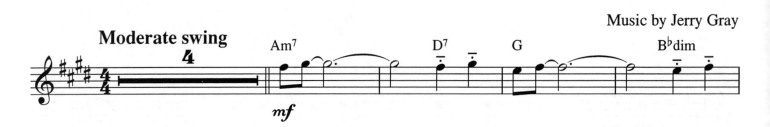

Demonstration

Backing

A String Of Pearls

Moderate swing

Music by Jerry Gray

28